MW00423705

SCOTT JAMES

The RISEN One

EXPERIENCING ALL OF
JESUS IN EASTER

FOREWORD BY MATT MASON

B&H
PUBLISHING
NASHVILLE, TENNESSEE

For my daughter, Bethan.

In Christ, love's redeeming work is done.

THE ORDER OF THINGS

—

FOREWORD

—

BY MATT MASON

As you probably know, the New Testament book called "the Acts of the Apostles" captures the rapid expansion of the gospel in the Roman Empire. Wherever the gospel went, Luke records, "there was great joy in that city" (Acts 8:8). Followers of the Way were marked by joy, hope, holiness, sincerity, generosity, and compassion. Because of their Spirit-empowered witness, an explosion of gospel power would be felt throughout the known world, ground zero of which was a bloody cross outside Jerusalem on Good Friday and an empty tomb on Easter Sunday. Despite the best laid efforts of Satanic powers and principalities, the world was turned upside down by this fledgling band of believers, who came to embrace an emphatic cry and creed that still rings in the air today: Christ has died, Christ has risen, Christ will come again!

To put it more personally, the apostle Paul would say it this way:

> The life I now live in the body, I live by faith in the Son of God, who loved me and gave himself for me. (Gal. 2:20)

He loved me and died for me—that's why I live this life of faith! Here's the upshot: If the knowledge of the gospel leads to a life of faith and perseverance and mission—and it does—then we cannot possibly know the Easter story too well. Enter, this little book. It's a tool meant to help you, perhaps along with family or friends, to remember the Story of the One who loved us and gave himself for us—to feel the still potent tremors of "It is Finished" and "He is Risen."

Scott James faithfully serves as an elder at The Church at Brook Hills. One of his areas of passion and gifting is to dazzle young hearts with the glory of Jesus and equip parents to do the same. This is why the devotional thoughts and discussion questions in this book, while useful to Christians of any maturity level, are written in a way to invite those who are young in faith or young in heart to join the conversation and gain understanding.

I hope the "great joy" that came to every city back in the time of Acts will be felt anew, right here and now, in every place where Holy Week is celebrated. I hope this little book will help you and yours find your voice in that ancient cry and creed: Christ has died, Christ has risen, Christ will come again. ✦

INTRODUCTION:
"HE IS RISEN!"

—

Easter is about the triumph of something unique to Christianity: the resurrection. Each year on Easter morning we have the privilege of celebrating Jesus Christ, the Risen One, who has conquered sin and death on our behalf. One way to fully experience the joy of that glorious Resurrection Day is to remember and rehearse the pathway that led Jesus to the cross, the grave, and beyond. As we reflect on the full scope of Jesus' life and ministry, it is my hope that we can grow in our appreciation of how He fulfilled God's plan to reconcile all things to Himself (Col. 1:20).

This book will give you a glimpse of the path Jesus walked as He made His way to the cross. The weekly devotionals pick up just after the arrival of the long-expected Savior, following Him as He reveals the good news of His kingdom, prepares Himself and His disciples for the sacrifice ahead, endures the agony of the cross, and triumphantly emerges from the grave in victory. Then, we'll see the Risen One unleash His people to testify in His name through the power of the Holy Spirit. You may recognize these themes as Christmastide, Epiphany, Lent, Easter, and Pentecost—seasons of the church calendar designed to guide us through the progression of God's unfolding plan of salvation.

The Risen One consists of twelve family-friendly weekly devotionals. Though the dates will change from year to year, if you use Easter Sunday as an anchor point and start this book ten weeks before, these devotionals will guide your family through the themes of Jesus' pathway to the cross in the months leading up to Easter, loosely coinciding with the seasons of the church calendar. Each week includes a key passage of Scripture, a brief explanation to help you follow along, discussion questions (and suggested answers) to help you connect with kids, an additional question to help you dig a little deeper, and a suggested prayer point based on the theme of the week. There are also suggested passages for daily readings, which will help round out the themes of each week's devotional. Taken together, the weekly devotionals and daily readings form a three-month reading plan that will be sure to enrich your Easter celebration.

Perhaps you're picking this book up because you're familiar with *The Expected One: Anticipating all of Jesus in the Advent.* While *The Risen One* serves as a companion to—and continuation of—*The Expected One*, you should also feel free to use it on its own. Either way, I pray that it serves you as a faithful guide into the riches of God's Word during the months leading up to Easter. ✦

PART ONE

CHRIST

Has

COME

WEEK 1

—

LUKE 2:25–35

There was a man in Jerusalem whose name was Simeon. This man was righteous and devout, looking forward to Israel's consolation, and the Holy Spirit was on him. It had been revealed to him by the Holy Spirit that he would not see death before he saw the Lord's Messiah. Guided by the Spirit, he entered the temple. When the parents brought in the child Jesus to perform for him what was customary under the law, Simeon took him up in his arms, praised God, and said,

Now, Master,
you can dismiss your servant in peace,
as you promised.
For my eyes have seen your salvation.
You have prepared it
in the presence of all peoples—
a light for revelation to the Gentiles
and glory to your people Israel.

His father and mother were amazed at what was being said about him. Then Simeon blessed them and told his mother Mary, "Indeed, this child is destined to cause the fall and rise of many in Israel and to be a sign that will be opposed—and a sword will pierce your own soul—that the thoughts of many hearts may be revealed."

Long ago, God made a glorious promise. To a wayward people, lost in rebellion and sin, God extended a gracious hand and promised rescue. A Savior would come—the consolation and comfort of Israel. Today's passage gives us a glimpse of what it must have been like for God's people as they awaited this Savior. Generation after generation, they had been expectantly watching for their Messiah, the one who would rescue them from their sin. In Luke 2, Simeon represents the hope of an entire nation. But now, as he holds this baby in his arms, Simeon sees God's promise fulfilled. Guided by the Holy Spirit, Simeon sees his salvation and rejoices—Hallelujah, Christ has come!

This long-expected Rescuer was Israel's consolation and glory, but His saving work would not be held in by Israel's borders. Simeon tells us this Savior would be a light to *all* nations. God's glorious promise of salvation had always been intended for Jews and Gentiles alike, and now Simeon rejoices at the arrival of Jesus, the Savior of the world. As he celebrates this joyful moment, however, Simeon reminds us that Jesus would accomplish this salvation through opposition and agony. Even as a baby, the shadow of the cross hung over Jesus' life; His saving sacrifice would be like a sword piercing his mother's very soul.

Simeon had been watching for the Messiah, but who actually led him to Jesus?

The Holy Spirit—God Himself led Simeon to recognize his Savior.

What do you think Simeon meant when he said Jesus would cause the rise and fall of many?

Those who trust in Jesus will be saved from sin and death, but whoever rejects Him will remain lost in those things.

Simeon told Mary a sword would pierce her soul. Why would he bring up a painful thing like that in the middle of a happy moment?

To show us that Jesus' sacrificial death was part of God's rescue plan from the very beginning.

After years of darkness, the Holy Spirit led Simeon to recognize the Light of the world. How is the Spirit leading you to see and share the light of Jesus?

_____

PRAYER POINT

Praise God for keeping His promise to send a Savior. Ask Him to help you be a part of His work as He reveals the light of salvation to all nations. ✦

DAILY READINGS

Psalm 24

Isaiah 9:1–7

Psalm 135

Jeremiah 31:1–14

Galatians 3:27–4:7

PART TWO

The

KINGDOM

REVEALED

WEEK 2

MATTHEW 2:1–12

After Jesus was born in Bethlehem of Judea in the days of King Herod, wise men from the east arrived in Jerusalem, saying, "Where is he who has been born king of the Jews? For we saw his star at its rising and have come to worship him."

When King Herod heard this, he was deeply disturbed, and all Jerusalem with him. So he assembled all the chief priests and scribes of the people and asked them where the Messiah would be born.

"In Bethlehem of Judea," they told him, "because this is what was written by the prophet:

> And you, Bethlehem, in the land of Judah,
> are by no means least among the rulers of
>   Judah:
> Because out of you will come a ruler who
>   will shepherd my people Israel."

Then Herod secretly summoned the wise men and asked them the exact time the star appeared. He sent them to Bethlehem and said, "Go and search carefully for the child. When you find him, report back to me so that I too can go and worship him."

After hearing the king, they went on their way. And there it was—the star they had seen at its rising. It led them until it came and stopped above the place where the child was. When they saw the star, they were overwhelmed with joy. Entering the house, they saw the child with Mary his mother, and falling to their knees, they worshiped him.

Then they opened their treasures and presented him with gifts: gold, frankincense, and myrrh. And being warned in a dream not to go back to Herod, they returned to their own country by another route.

The arrival of the Savior was very good news, but what's the point of good news if it isn't shared? During Jesus' early life and ministry, God shared the good news of His arrival in wonderful and surprising ways, drawing people to the Rescuer and displaying His glory. Over the next few weeks as we make our way to the cross, we'll walk through stories of God revealing that His kingdom had come into the world in the person of Jesus Christ. One of the earliest and most astonishing of these examples is the visit of the wise men. Whereas Simeon held the newborn king as a one-month-old, Jesus was probably closer to one or two years old by the time the wise men made it to His house.

These wise men were not from among God's people, but they knew enough of Scripture to know God had promised a coming king. How did the wise men know where to find this king? The God who created the stars and controls the heavens led them with a miraculous sign. When God chose to bring the wise men to Jesus, He was announcing that the nations would be granted the privilege of knowing the true king. But even as outsiders came worshipping and bearing gifts fit for a king, the people who should have been glad to hear of Jesus' arrival ended up opposing Him. But God's plan would not be stopped. The wise men's quest shows us the kingdom of God has been revealed to the world, and God is still drawing people to Himself in miraculous ways.

Would the wise men have been able to find Jesus without God's help?

No, God led the way. God loves pointing people to His Son, Jesus.

What do the gifts of gold, frankincense, and myrrh tell us about Jesus?

These were treasured gifts that tell us the wise men recognized Jesus' kingly nature.

Why do you think Herod was unhappy about Jesus' arrival?

Because he thought of himself as the king of the Jews, and he didn't want to give up his power to a new king.

When God brought the wise men into the presence of King Jesus, they were overwhelmed with joy as they worshipped him. How is your life marked by joyful worship?

PRAYER POINT

Give thanks to God for inviting all nations to come and see King Jesus. Ask His Spirit to change hearts and bring joyful praise all around the world. ✦

DAILY READINGS

PSALM 19

ISAIAH 60:1–6

PSALM 72

1 KINGS 10:1–13

REVELATION 7:9–12

WEEK 3

—

MARK 1:1–11

The beginning of the gospel of Jesus Christ, the Son of God. As it is written in Isaiah the prophet:

> See, I am sending my messenger ahead
>   of you;
> he will prepare your way.
> A voice of one crying out in the wilderness:
> Prepare the way for the Lord;
>   make his paths straight!

John came baptizing in the wilderness and proclaiming a baptism of repentance for the forgiveness of sins. The whole Judean countryside and all the people of Jerusalem were going out to him, and they were baptized by him in the Jordan River, confessing their sins. John wore a camel-hair garment with a leather belt around his waist and ate locusts and wild honey.

He proclaimed, "One who is more powerful than I am is coming after me. I am not worthy to stoop down and untie the strap of his sandals. I baptize you with water, but he will baptize you with the Holy Spirit."

In those days Jesus came from Nazareth in Galilee and was baptized in the Jordan by John. As soon as he came up out of the water, he saw the heavens being torn open and the Spirit descending on him like a dove. And a voice came from heaven: "You are my beloved Son; with you I am well-pleased."

When the time came for Jesus to put His rescue plan in motion, He got a special introduction from a man in camel-hair clothes. God had chosen Jesus' cousin, John, to go before Him and prepare the path ahead. John sure could draw a crowd, but he knew his job was to point others to Jesus. John had a message for the people: turn away from sin and seek forgiveness from God. But he didn't stop there—John didn't just have a message to deliver; he had a Savior to introduce. When Jesus arrived, John declared, "Here is the Lamb of God, who takes away the sin of the world!" (John 1:29). God's people had strayed far from Him, cast out of the garden and into the wilderness. In order to bring them back, God sent John wandering in from the wilderness, telling people they could come home in Christ.

Even though God was faithful to send His messenger ahead of Jesus to proclaim His arrival (just as He had promised He would), the people didn't have to take John's word for it. As John ushered in the start of Jesus' ministry by baptizing Him, God Himself announced out loud that Jesus was His beloved Son while the Holy Spirit descended on Him like a dove. Here, the Father, the Son, and the Holy Spirit declared together that the long-awaited time of salvation had come. "The time is fulfilled, and the kingdom of God has come near. Repent and believe the good news!" (Mark 1:15).

Why was John calling on people to confess their sin?

Because in order to be found by God, He first asks us to admit that we've wandered away from Him.

At Jesus' baptism, what was so special about the voice from heaven and the dove?

This is one of the places in the Bible where we see the Trinity—God the Father, Jesus the Son, and the Holy Spirit. The Bible tells us God is three persons in one.

When John spoke to lost people, he had the privilege of pointing to Jesus and saying, "Look who's here!" How can we join John in pointing to the Savior?

Parents, talk with your children about the people in your life with whom you have the privilege of sharing the good news of Jesus.

Though Jesus was without sin, He chose to receive John's "baptism of repentance for the forgiveness of sins." What is so significant about this picture of a sinless Savior identifying with fallen sinners?

PRAYER POINT

Spend some time confessing sin and asking God to help you turn from it. Then, praise God that forgiveness is available in Christ. ✦

DAILY READINGS

ISAIAH 40:1–11

PSALM 2

EXODUS 12

PSALM 51

ISAIAH 42:1–9

WEEK 4

—

JOHN 2:1–11

On the third day a wedding took place in Cana of Galilee. Jesus' mother was there, and Jesus and his disciples were invited to the wedding as well. When the wine ran out, Jesus' mother told him, "They don't have any wine."

"What has this concern of yours to do with me, woman?" Jesus asked. "My hour has not yet come."

"Do whatever he tells you," his mother told the servants.

Now six stone water jars had been set there for Jewish purification. Each contained twenty or thirty gallons.

"Fill the jars with water," Jesus told them. So they filled them to the brim. Then he said to them, "Now draw some out and take it to the headwaiter." And they did.

When the headwaiter tasted the water (after it had become wine), he did not know where it came from—though the servants who had drawn the water knew. He called the groom and told him, "Everyone sets out the fine wine first, then, after people are drunk, the inferior. But you have kept the fine wine until now."

Jesus did this, the first of his signs, in Cana of Galilee. He revealed his glory, and his disciples believed in him.

There was a time early in Jesus' ministry when He had already been announced as the Son of God, but the glorious news of His arrival had not yet been shared with everyone. In His perfect timing, Jesus began revealing His presence to certain groups of people. Sometimes He did this through words alone, while other times He chose to give a demonstration of His glory and power. This week's passage is one such demonstration—the first of His signs to show people that He was indeed the expected Messiah. The scene is a wedding feast. It's a party, but it's a party with a problem: they've run out of wine! So, prompted by His mother, Jesus stepped up and did something impossible. He took six huge water jars, and, to everyone's astonishment, He miraculously turned the water into wine.

Why did Jesus do this? Turning water into wine was not just a cute party trick; it was intended to demonstrate that Jesus was able to do things only God could do. Jesus wasn't just claiming to be the Messiah. He was showing it—with miraculous power! The passage makes Jesus' purpose crystal clear: "He revealed his glory, and his disciples believed in him." The long-awaited Messiah was really here! This was His first miracle, but all throughout the Gospels, Jesus' signs and wonders were a part of His plan to help people believe He truly was God. Every one of His miracles was intended to proclaim a truth and ask a question.

The truth: "I am the Messiah."
The question: "Will you believe in Me?"

When Jesus turned the water into wine, was it just a trick or an illusion?

No, Jesus actually transformed one thing into another. It was a true miracle.

How did this show that Jesus is God?

Because God created all things, He alone has control over all things. At Cana, Jesus gave us a glimpse of His control over nature.

What do Jesus' miracles tell us about the kind of faith God asks us to have?

He does not call us to blind faith—He gives powerful proof that He is worth believing!

What does it look like, daily, to believe that Jesus truly is the miraculous Messiah? How does this belief affect the way you are living your life?

PRAYER POINT

Praise God for the glory He has revealed to us in Jesus Christ, our Savior. ✦

DAILY READINGS

Amos 9:11–15

Isaiah 25

Psalm 77:11–15

Hebrews 2:2–4

Revelation 19:5–9

WEEK 5

LUKE 7:1–10

When he had concluded saying all this to the people who were listening, he entered Capernaum. A centurion's servant, who was highly valued by him, was sick and about to die. When the centurion heard about Jesus, he sent some Jewish elders to him, requesting him to come and save the life of his servant. When they reached Jesus, they pleaded with him earnestly, saying, "He is worthy for you to grant this, because he loves our nation and has built us a synagogue."

Jesus went with them, and when he was not far from the house, the centurion sent friends to tell him, "Lord, don't trouble yourself, since I am not worthy to have you come under my roof. That is why I didn't even consider myself worthy to come to you. But say the word, and my servant will be healed. For I too am a man placed under authority, having soldiers under my command. I say to this one, 'Go,' and he goes; and to another, 'Come,' and he comes; and to my servant, 'Do this,' and he does it."

Jesus heard this and was amazed at him, and turning to the crowd following him, he said, "I tell you, I have not found so great a faith even in Israel." When those who had been sent returned to the house, they found the servant in good health.

As Jesus traveled around, ministering to people and calling them to follow Him, it made sense that He would start with His own Jewish community. After all, the people of Israel—the descendants of Abraham himself—had been the ones who first received God's promise that a Rescuer would come. Now, after generations of watching and waiting, that promise had been fulfilled, and the Rescuer stood among them. But as Jesus made His way around, sharing the good news of His arrival, an amazing part of God's plan began to unfold: people from outside of Israel began coming to Jesus, too! In this week's passage, a commander (or centurion) in the Roman army sensed Jesus' power and sought help on behalf of a dying servant.

This centurion was a man who understood authority—he had the power of the Roman army at his command. Rather than making him proud and arrogant, however, being in charge of other people made this centurion humble and helped him recognize true power when he saw it in Jesus. God had prepared this man by giving him a heart that cared for others, an appreciation of Jesus' unique worth, and the belief that Jesus was compassionate. He saw Jesus' authority and had faith that He would use it to save. For His part, Jesus was "amazed" by this kind of faith. In Matthew's description of the encounter, he includes an astonishing detail: Jesus told His followers that, "many will come from east and west to share the banquet with Abraham, Isaac, and Jacob in the kingdom of heaven" (Matthew 8:11). As Jesus revealed His kingdom, He made it clear that the Jews (Abraham's offspring) were not the only ones invited. The Roman centurion in this passage shows us that Jesus will welcome anyone who trusts in Him, no matter where they are from. Jesus came for the whole world.

Jesus was willing to stop everything to go visit a dying man. Does that tell us anything about what Jesus is like?

It shows us that Jesus has compassion for those in need.

What did the centurion mean when he said Jesus only had to "say the word" for the dying servant to be healed?

He knew that Jesus' word had power, even over life itself.

Was the inclusion of non-Jewish people in the kingdom a new part of God's plan?

No, it had been God's plan from the beginning. Israel was God's chosen nation, but it was always meant to be a light for all nations!

The centurion was a leader who used his authority to help people. If there are any areas in your life where God has given you a leadership role, how are you using that responsibility to care for others? What are some ways you might better reflect the ways Jesus handles authority?

PRAYER POINT

Ask God to grant you an amazing faith— faith that sees Jesus clearly, trusts Him wholeheartedly, shares Him impartially, and loves others compassionately. ✦

DAILY READINGS

GENESIS 12:1–3

PSALM 67

ISAIAH 49:1–13

PSALM 103

EPHESIANS 3:1–12

PART THREE

The

DAYS

of

PREPARATION

WEEK 6

—

JOHN 3:1–17

There was a man from the Pharisees named Nicodemus, a ruler of the Jews. This man came to him at night and said, "Rabbi, we know that you are a teacher who has come from God, for no one could perform these signs you do unless God were with him."

Jesus replied, "Truly I tell you, unless someone is born again, he cannot see the kingdom of God."

"How can anyone be born when he is old?" Nicodemus asked him. "Can he enter his mother's womb a second time and be born?"

Jesus answered, "Truly I tell you, unless someone is born of water and the Spirit, he cannot enter the kingdom of God. Whatever is born of the flesh is flesh, and whatever is born of the Spirit is spirit. Do not be amazed that I told you that you must be born again. The wind blows where it pleases, and you hear its sound, but you don't know where it comes from or where it is going. So it is with everyone born of the Spirit."

"How can these things be?" asked Nicodemus.

"Are you a teacher of Israel and don't know these things?" Jesus replied. "Truly I tell you, we speak what we know and we testify to what we have seen, but you do not accept our testimony. If I have told you about earthly things and you don't believe, how will you believe if I tell you about heavenly things? No one has ascended into heaven except the one who descended from heaven—the Son of Man.

"Just as Moses lifted up the snake in the wilderness, so the Son of Man must be lifted up, so that everyone who believes in him may have eternal life. For God loved the world in this way: He gave his one and only Son, so that everyone who believes in him will not perish but have eternal life. For God did not send his Son into the world to condemn the world, but to save the world through him."

So far in His ministry, we have seen Jesus calling on people to believe that He is the Savior sent from God. His arrival has been announced and His kingdom revealed. His words and His miraculous works have been challenging people with the question, "Will you believe I am the king? Will you come into my kingdom?" Well, here in John 3 we have one of the Jewish leaders meeting with Jesus and learning what it truly means to do just that. Nicodemus had been raised to believe that being a part of God's kingdom was based on the family you were born into here on earth. Jesus tells Nicodemus that a spiritual birth, not a physical one, is needed to enter God's kingdom. Unless you've been born again, you can't even truly see the kingdom of God.

When Nicodemus asks Jesus to tell him more about what it means to be born again, Jesus uses two illustrations to help him understand. First, the wind is a picture of God moving in the world, bringing new life through the work of the Holy Spirit. Like wind rustling leaves, we don't always see the Spirit moving, but we can see and hear its effects. When the Spirit of God brings new life, we awaken to the kingdom of God and are ushered into it. The second illustration is of a snake statue lifted up on a pole, which is a story from Israel's past about a time when God asked His people to look up at this emblem, and in so doing, be miraculously saved from the consequences of their sin. This story may sound odd, but it teaches us that new life in God is possible only through faith in Jesus, who would soon be lifted up on a cross to take away our sin.

Taken together, these two illustrations help us see that to enter into God's kingdom, we must be given new life by His Spirit and look up to Christ in faith as our Savior. Even as He spoke with Nicodemus, Jesus was preparing Himself for the sacrifice He would make to save anyone who believes in Him.

Why did Jesus expect Nicodemus to know about the Holy Spirit who brings new life?

Because Nicodemus was a teacher of the Old Testament, which often spoke of our need for a new heart and new spiritual life; for example, see Ezekiel 36:26.

If Jesus is God, why did He call Himself the Son of Man?

This was another name for the Messiah. It reminds us that Jesus is fully God and fully man.

In verse 16, what made God want to send His Son to save us from sin?

Because He loves us!

The Father sends, the Spirit moves, and with our newly awakened eyes we see Jesus, high and lifted up as the Savior of the world. Take a moment to reflect on how each person of the Trinity is active in your salvation.

PRAYER POINT

Praise God for loving us enough to send His one and only Son to die in our place, and for giving us His Spirit who brings us new life. ✦

DAILY READINGS

NUMBERS 21:4–9

PSALM 136

EZEKIEL 36:22–30

JOHN 6:35–40

TITUS 3:4–7

WEEK 7

—

LUKE 7:36–50

Then one of the Pharisees invited him to eat with him. He entered the Pharisee's house and reclined at the table. And a woman in the town who was a sinner found out that Jesus was reclining at the table in the Pharisee's house. She brought an alabaster jar of perfume and stood behind him at his feet, weeping, and began to wash his feet with her tears. She wiped his feet with her hair, kissing them and anointing them with the perfume.

When the Pharisee who had invited him saw this, he said to himself, "This man, if he were a prophet, would know who and what kind of woman this is who is touching him—she's a sinner!"

Jesus replied to him, "Simon, I have something to say to you."

He said, "Say it, teacher."

"A creditor had two debtors. One owed five hundred denarii, and the other fifty. Since they could not pay it back, he graciously forgave them both. So, which of them will love him more?"

Simon answered, "I suppose the one he forgave more."

"You have judged correctly," he told him. Turning to the woman, he said to Simon, "Do you see this woman? I entered your house; you gave me no water for my feet, but she, with her tears, has washed my feet and wiped them with her hair. You gave me no kiss, but she hasn't stopped kissing my feet since I came in. You didn't anoint my head with olive oil, but she has anointed my feet with perfume. Therefore I tell you, her many sins have been forgiven; that's why she loved much. But the one who is forgiven little, loves little." Then he said to her, "Your sins are forgiven."

Those who were at the table with him began to say among themselves, "Who is this man who even forgives sins?"

And he said to the woman, "Your faith has saved you. Go in peace."

Asking for help can be a difficult thing. Even when we know we really need it, sometimes we're still hesitant to ask. We think we can handle things ourselves, and we don't want to look weak or incapable. That's just pride getting in the way. Jesus came to confront that kind of pride. Knowing that we could never overcome the problem of sin, Jesus came alongside to tell us, "Stop trying to save yourself—just turn away from sin and trust in Me!" This week's passage shows us two very different responses to Jesus' loving invitation. The woman in the story was known all over town for her sin, while Simon the Pharisee was an upstanding religious leader. Isn't it surprising, then, that Jesus connected more with her than He did with Simon? The difference was that she knew she was broken, and that Jesus could make her whole; Simon didn't even seem willing to admit he needed help.

The woman understood her great need and she was determined to seek help from the Savior who freely offered to give it. She didn't care what others thought about her (which is good because, sure enough, Simon ridiculed her). It was as if Simon called her a big sinner and she responded, "I know! That's why I need a big Savior!" She was driven by her love for Jesus and a desperate need for His compassionate grace. As this woman's faith brought her weeping to the feet of Jesus, He declared her sins forgiven. Those same feet would soon be pierced by nails as Jesus secured that forgiveness on the cross.

At one point in this story, Jesus knew what Simon was thinking even though Simon hadn't spoken out loud. How is that possible?

Because Jesus is God, and He knows all things.

Even though he didn't act like it, do you think Simon had a sin problem too?

Yes, but he was unwilling to admit it. Many of the religious leaders thought they were already good enough for God, so they didn't think they needed Jesus.

When we realize we've disobeyed God, it may make us feel sad. What can we do if that's the case?

God tells us that if we confess our sins to Him, He will be faithful to forgive us; see 1 John 1:9.

If we realize we've disobeyed God, and it *doesn't* make us sad, should we be concerned about that? What kinds of things can dull or quench our sense of conviction over sin?

PRAYER POINT

Tell God how grateful you are that He came to save sinners like us. Thank Him for the forgiveness He grants to those who confess they need Jesus and put their faith in Him. ✦

DAILY READINGS

PSALM 4

ISAIAH 12

PROVERBS 28:13

PSALM 107:1–9

1 JOHN 1

WEEK 8

—

LUKE 9:18–27

While he was praying in private and his disciples were with him, he asked them, "Who do the crowds say that I am?"

They answered, "John the Baptist; others, Elijah; still others, that one of the ancient prophets has come back."

"But you," he asked them, "who do you say that I am?"

Peter answered, "God's Messiah."

But he strictly warned and instructed them to tell this to no one, saying, "It is necessary that the Son of Man suffer many things and be rejected by the elders, chief priests, and scribes, be killed, and be raised the third day."

Then he said to them all, "If anyone wants to follow after me, let him deny himself, take up his cross daily, and follow me. For whoever wants to save his life will lose it, but whoever loses his life because of me will save it. For what does it benefit someone if he gains the whole world, and yet loses or forfeits himself? For whoever is ashamed of me and my words, the Son of Man will be ashamed of him when he comes in his glory and that of the Father and the holy angels. Truly I tell you, there are some standing here who will not taste death until they see the kingdom of God."

With each passing day, Jesus stepped closer and closer to the completion of His great rescue mission. As He prepared for the end of His earthly days, Jesus pulled His disciples aside to make sure they truly grasped what was happening. People often misunderstood who Jesus was, so He made it unmistakably clear to His closest followers—He told them exactly who He was, what His mission would require, and the path they would be asked to walk after He was gone. While rumors of Jesus' real identity swirled around them, Peter made the good confession: Jesus was indeed God's Messiah, the Savior sent to rescue us from our sin.

Based on that confession, Jesus helped His disciples see the sad and wonderful truth of how He would accomplish His great rescue—

the Son of Man would suffer, die on the cross in our place, and then, as glorious proof of His victory over sin, He would be raised from the dead. This was why He came; this was what He had been calling people to believe all along. And for those who would believe, Jesus described what walking with Him looks like: we must deny ourselves, take up our cross daily, and follow Him. We die to self and live with Christ. In a world where we are constantly told to be true to ourselves, self-denial may sound like an odd thing to command. But there can be only one king of our lives—will it be us or Jesus? To deny yourself doesn't mean you are mean to yourself or that you hate yourself, rather, it is simply to admit that you can't save yourself; you need Jesus to be your rescuing king. We all do.

After Jesus asked about the crowds, He asked His disciples directly, "who do you say that I am?" What's so important about this follow-up question?

Jesus is calling for a personal response from each and every person. Our eternity depends on it.

Why do you think Jesus said we have to take up our cross daily? How can we die to self more than once?

Because following Jesus means we are willing to trust and obey Him not only on the day He saves us, but every single day after that, too.

Is following Jesus all "death and denial"? What reward does Jesus tell us about in this passage?

Whoever follows Jesus and is not ashamed of Him will be saved from the penalty of sin and will be with Jesus forever after He returns in glory.

Think about the paradox of this passage: if we try to hang on to our life, we will lose it, but if we entrust ourselves to Jesus, we will find eternal life in Him. In what ways are we tempted to take control of our own lives?

PRAYER POINT

Ask God to grant you daily faith in Him—a faith that causes you to willingly set aside your own way as you trust and obey the Risen Savior. ✦

DAILY READINGS

PSALM 1

ZECHARIAH 14:1–11

PSALM 119:89–104

LUKE 9:28–36

GALATIANS 2:16–21

WEEK 9

—

MARK 10:35–45

James and John, the sons of Zebedee, approached him and said, "Teacher, we want you to do whatever we ask you."

"What do you want me to do for you?" he asked them.

They answered him, "Allow us to sit at your right and at your left in your glory."

Jesus said to them, "You don't know what you're asking. Are you able to drink the cup I drink or to be baptized with the baptism I am baptized with?"

"We are able," they told him.

Jesus said to them, "You will drink the cup I drink, and you will be baptized with the baptism I am baptized with. But to sit at my right or left is not mine to give; instead, it is for those for whom it has been prepared."

When the ten disciples heard this, they began to be indignant with James and John. Jesus called them over and said to them, "You know that those who are regarded as rulers of the Gentiles lord it over them, and those in high positions act as tyrants over them. But it is not so among you. On the contrary, whoever wants to become great among you will be your servant, and whoever wants to be first among you will be a slave to all. For even the Son of Man did not come to be served, but to serve, and to give his life as a ransom for many."

THE WAY TO THE CROSS

Even if the disciples were clear on who Jesus was—God's Messiah—they still sometimes struggled to understand His ways (we can all be like that sometimes, too, can't we?). Jesus had told them of the coming glory of the kingdom of God and two of the disciples couldn't help but get a little ahead of themselves. They wanted to lay claim to some of those future rewards as soon as possible. You can almost hear the patience in Jesus' voice as He gently puts things in perspective for them. Before they claimed the crown of glory, there would first need to be a time of suffering and service.

The suffering in store was the penalty we deserved for our sin—our rebellion against God. But once again, Jesus was reminding His followers that He was the Lamb of God, sent to die in our place. We would still receive the glory (being saved from our sin, brought into the family of God, and eventually raised to life in resurrection), but Jesus Himself would be the one to pay the entrance fee. He would drink the cup of God's wrath toward sin, and in His death, burial, and resurrection, we would be baptized into new life with Him. The disciples wanted to make reservations for the most glorious seats in God's kingdom, but here Jesus was telling them that when they are united with Him, they no longer need to grasp for glory—it is freely and eternally theirs in Him! By dying in our place, Jesus would set the example of selfless service on behalf of others, an example He calls us to follow as we humbly receive His gift of salvation and seek to serve others in a similarly humble way.

Does it surprise you that Jesus' closest friends
were scheming for places of high honor?

*Parents, help your children see that even those who are close
to Jesus can be tempted to use Him for their own purposes.*

Does the humility Jesus talks about in this
passage come naturally to us, or is it a struggle?

*Often, considering other people's needs before
our own is a struggle. Jesus gives us the best
example of serving others in selflessness.*

What does this passage mean when it says Jesus
gave His life as a "ransom" for others?

*A ransom is a payment made to set
someone free; we were held prisoner by sin,
but Jesus paid the price of death to set us free.*

The Son of Man did not come to be served, but to serve. As you follow Jesus, how is this principle playing out in your life?

PRAYER POINT

Thank God for sending Jesus to step in and ransom us from the penalty of sin we deserved. Ask Him to give you a humble heart that seeks to serve others sacrificially, as an imitation of Jesus. ✦

DAILY READINGS

PSALM 75

ISAIAH 51:1–6, 17–23

PSALM 130

JEREMIAH 25:15–28

PHILIPPIANS 2:1–11

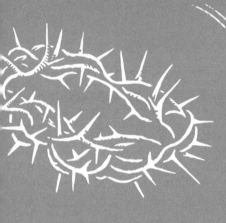

PART FOUR

The

DEATH

of

CHRIST

WEEK 10

MARK 15:20–39

After they had mocked him, they stripped him of the purple robe and put his clothes on him. They led him out to crucify him. They forced a man coming in from the country, who was passing by, to carry Jesus' cross. He was Simon of Cyrene, the father of Alexander and Rufus.

They brought Jesus to the place called *Golgotha* (which means Place of the Skull). They tried to give him wine mixed with myrrh, but he did not take it.

Then they crucified him and divided his clothes, casting lots for them to decide what each would get. Now it was nine in the morning when they crucified him. The inscription of the charge written against him was: THE KING OF THE JEWS. They crucified two criminals with him, one on his right and one on his left.

Those who passed by were yelling insults at him, shaking their heads, and saying, "Ha! The one who would destroy the temple and rebuild it in three days, save yourself by coming down from the cross!" In the same way, the chief priests with the scribes were mocking him among themselves and saying, "He saved others, but he cannot save himself! Let the Messiah, the King of Israel, come down now from the cross, so that we may see and believe." Even those who were crucified with him taunted him.

When it was noon, darkness came over the whole land until three in the afternoon. And at three Jesus cried out with a loud voice, *"Eloi, Eloi, lemá sabachtháni?"* which is translated, "My God, my God, why have you abandoned me?"

When some of those standing there heard this, they said, "See, he's calling for Elijah."

Someone ran and filled a sponge with sour wine, fixed it on a stick, offered him a drink, and said, "Let's see if Elijah comes to take him down."

Jesus let out a loud cry and breathed his last. Then the curtain of the temple was torn in two from top to bottom. When the centurion, who was standing opposite him, saw the way he breathed his last, he said, "Truly this man was the Son of God!"

If you're following along with the daily readings, this week you'll walk along with Jesus through the events of Holy Week—the week leading up to Jesus' death on the cross. But the passage we'll zoom in on this week tells us about Good Friday. Good Friday is what we call the day Jesus died on the cross in our place. You may be wondering how the day of Jesus' death could possibly be a good day. It certainly involved more suffering than we could ever comprehend, but, as we'll see, Jesus' death was the decisive moment in the rescue plan that had been promised long ago.

After traveling into Jerusalem, Jesus challenged the religious leaders of the day in a way that made it clear He was the Savior sent from God to rescue people from sin. This irritated some of the religious leaders, who thought they had figured out their own way to please God. Jesus was betrayed, arrested, beaten, subjected to a mockery of a trial, and then sentenced to death. As Jesus hung dying on the cross, He cried out in agony to God and then breathed His last. His death made a way for any who would believe in Him to be reconciled to God. Some of those who were watching His agony realized He really was the Son of God, but many people continued to mock and reject Him.

Did Jesus deserve the punishment He received on the cross?

No, He never sinned and did not deserve to die. We deserve that death, but Jesus stepped in and took it in our place.

Was Jesus taken to the cross against His will?

No, He sacrificed Himself willingly. It was for this purpose that He came; see John 10:18.

What was so special about the curtain in the temple being torn in two?

The curtain represented the fact that our sin separated us from God. The curtain being torn meant that Jesus' death opened the way into God's presence.

Imagine the abandonment Jesus felt when He cried out on the cross, "My God, my God, why have you abandoned me?" How does it make you feel to know that it was your sin that brought that anguish upon Him? Though the thought of Jesus' anguish may cause you sorrow, how does it feel to know He endured such agony with joy—joy in the fact that His work would reconcile you forever to the Father (see Hebrews 12:2)?

PRAYER POINT

Praise God for sending His Son to die in your place, willingly taking the punishment you deserve upon Himself. Thank Jesus for providing salvation in this way. ✦

DAILY READINGS

LUKE 19:28–40

JOHN 12:20–50

LUKE 22:7–23

MARK 14:32–50

MATTHEW 27:11–25

PART FIVE

CHRIST

Is

RISEN

WEEK 11

—

MATTHEW 28:1–10

After the Sabbath, as the first day of the week was dawning, Mary Magdalene and the other Mary went to view the tomb. There was a violent earthquake, because an angel of the Lord descended from heaven and approached the tomb. He rolled back the stone and was sitting on it. His appearance was like lightning, and his clothing was as white as snow. The guards were so shaken by fear of him that they became like dead men.

The angel told the women, "Don't be afraid, because I know you are looking for Jesus who was crucified. He is not here. For he has risen, just as he said. Come and see the place where he lay. Then go quickly and tell his disciples, 'He has risen from the dead and indeed he is going ahead of you to Galilee; you will see him there.' Listen, I have told you."

So, departing quickly from the tomb with fear and great joy, they ran to tell his disciples the news. Just then Jesus met them and said, "Greetings!" They came up, took hold of his feet, and worshiped him. Then Jesus told them, "Do not be afraid. Go and tell my brothers to leave for Galilee, and they will see me there."

Leading up to the cross, Jesus had prepared His disciples to be ready for the sacrifice He was about to make. And He hadn't just prepared them for His death—He also pointed them beyond that, to the new life He would see on the other side of the grave. But no matter how many times Jesus had told them death would not be the end of His story, this was a hard thing for His friends to wrap their minds around. Should they really expect a dead man to come back to life? Through His miraculous signs and wonders, Jesus had given them plenty of reason to take Him at His word, but after witnessing His agonizing death on Good Friday, Jesus' followers were full of fear and doubt. They were being asked to believe the impossible, and it seems like they just weren't up to it.

Thankfully, God specializes in the impossible—time and time again, He accomplishes marvelous works that are simply too good to be true, and then He grants us the faith to truly believe. That's exactly what the women encountered on Sunday morning when they went to Jesus' tomb to prepare His body for final burial. With a boom and a flash, they found themselves standing in front of an empty tomb and a shining man, who told them the most wonderful thing: "He is not here. For he has risen, just as he said." Astonishing! Even better, as they rushed back to tell the others, the women came face-to-face with the Risen One Himself! As they fell down and worshipped Jesus, the pain of seeing Him suffer on the cross must have felt like an old memory. That pain wasn't completely gone, but now on Easter morning they were seeing things in a new light—a cross declaring victory over sin, and an empty tomb proclaiming death itself had been defeated. God had kept His promise after all.

Why do you think the angel told the women not to be afraid?

> *Parents, help your children see how truly astounding this event must have been to experience. An open tomb, a missing body, a heavenly being—this was not a normal scene!*

After the angel reminded the women that this was exactly what Jesus had said would happen, what was their response?

> *They believed. They may not have understood everything going on yet, and they were still a little afraid, but they ran with "great joy" to tell the others.*

What was their immediate response when they met the Risen Jesus?

> *They worshipped Him.*

How does the resurrection of Jesus Christ affect the way you live your life today?

_____

PRAYER POINT

Praise God for the astounding truth that death has been defeated forever by the resurrection of Jesus. Thank God that, though faith in Jesus, we gain the reward of eternal life. ✦

DAILY READINGS

PSALM 110

ISAIAH 53

PSALM 126

1 CORINTHIANS 15

ROMANS 10:4–13

PART SIX

The

CHURCH

ALIVE

WEEK 12

ACTS 1:1–14

I wrote the first narrative, Theophilus, about all that Jesus began to do and teach until the day he was taken up, after he had given instructions through the Holy Spirit to the apostles he had chosen. After he had suffered, he also presented himself alive to them by many convincing proofs, appearing to them over a period of forty days and speaking about the kingdom of God.

While he was with them, he commanded them not to leave Jerusalem, but to wait for the Father's promise. "Which," he said, "you have heard me speak about; for John baptized with water, but you will be baptized with the Holy Spirit in a few days."

So when they had come together, they asked him, "Lord, are you restoring the kingdom to Israel at this time?"

He said to them, "It is not for you to know times or periods that the Father has set by his own authority. But you will receive power when the Holy Spirit has come on you, and you will be my witnesses in Jerusalem, in all Judea and Samaria, and to the ends of the earth."

After he had said this, he was taken up as they were watching, and a cloud took him out of their sight. While he was going, they were gazing into heaven, and suddenly two men in white clothes stood by them. They said, "Men of Galilee, why do you stand looking up into heaven? This same Jesus, who has been taken from you into heaven, will come in the same way that you have seen him going into heaven."

Then they returned to Jerusalem from the Mount of Olives, which is near Jerusalem—a Sabbath day's journey away. When they arrived, they went to the room upstairs where they were staying: Peter, John, James, Andrew, Philip, Thomas, Bartholomew, Matthew, James the son of Alphaeus, Simon the Zealot, and Judas the son of James. They all were continually united in prayer, along with the women, including Mary the mother of Jesus, and his brothers.

Christ is risen! Now what? In our final passage, we get to see how God planned to continue His work by bringing His church to life by the power of the Holy Spirit. The Spirit's coming was promised beforehand by Jesus and is another example of how God's rescue plan has always involved all three persons of the Trinity: God the Father sending a Savior, Jesus the Son providing the way of salvation through His perfect life and sacrificial death in our place, and the Holy Spirit working in our hearts to bring new life and guide us into truth. All throughout Jesus' earthly ministry, He had been working in perfect unison with the Father and the Spirit to bring about the salvation they had planned long ago. Now, having completed His work on the earth, it was time for Jesus to return to heaven. His followers would not be left on their own, though. Jesus once again promised the Holy Spirit would come, giving the church the power to continue God's work in the world. Fueled by the Spirit, God's people would be an outward-facing witness of God's glory and the salvation He offers. Jesus tells His disciples that the Spirit will lead them across borders, proclaiming the kingdom of God to all people groups—even to the ends of the earth.

After telling His disciples these things, Jesus—the Risen One—rose one more time as He was taken up into heaven. Just in case the disciples were too shocked to process what was going on, two angels appeared and told them that Jesus would one day return in the same way. By promising them Jesus would come again, it was almost as if the angels were reminding the disciples that they had work to do while awaiting His return. He had just given them a mission. United in prayer, the disciples gathered to wait for the coming of the Holy Spirit. Sure enough, a few days later, the Holy Spirit filled them with power and sent them out into the world to proclaim the good news of Jesus (Acts 2). This is the same mission you and I get to be a part of today. While we wait for Jesus' return, we get to glorify God by telling the world about our Risen Savior and the salvation He provides.

Why was it important for the disciples to wait for the Holy Spirit before heading out on mission?

Because we need God's power to accomplish His mission.

Do you think the disciples may have felt overwhelmed when Jesus told them they would be His witnesses all over the world?

Parents, help your children see that when God calls us to do something hard, He will always be with us to help us through it. We don't need to be afraid of attempting big things for God!

What kind of example did the disciples set for us when they were waiting on the Holy Spirit to come?

They trusted Jesus, obeyed His command, and remained united in prayer. We can all strive to follow their example here.

As you live out the mission God has called you to, are there any areas where you are not relying on the Spirit of God?

PRAYER POINT

Ask God to give you a heart that longs for the return of Jesus and a life that relies on His power as you boldly witness for Him. ✦

DAILY READINGS

PSALM 47

JOHN 15:26–16:11

MATTHEW 28: 16–20

ACTS 2

COLOSSIANS 1:9–23

EASTER FAMILY MEMORIES

EASTER FAMILY MEMORIES

EASTER FAMILY MEMORIES

EASTER FAMILY MEMORIES

EASTER FAMILY MEMORIES

EASTER FAMILY MEMORIES

EASTER FAMILY MEMORIES

EASTER FAMILY MEMORIES

EASTER FAMILY MEMORIES

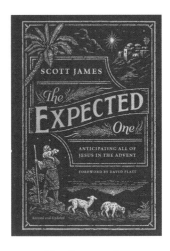

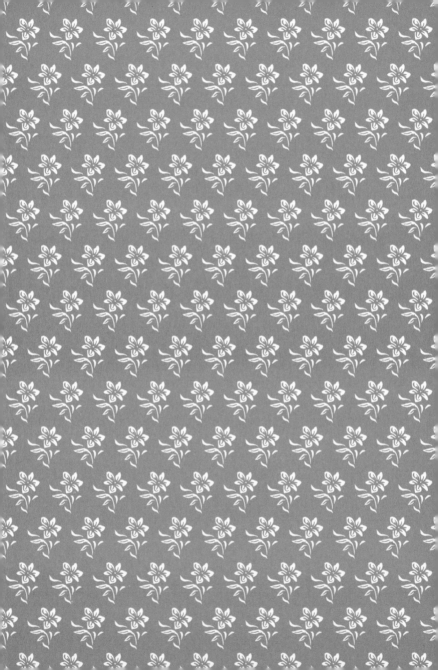